the

book

of

ten

PITT POETRY SERIES

Ed Ochester, Editor

the

book

of

ten

SUSAN WOOD

UNIVERSITY OF PITTSBURGH PRESS

Published by the University of Pittsburgh Press, Pittsburgh, Pa., 15260

Manufactured in the United States of America
Printed on acid-free paper
10 9 8 7 6 5 4 3 2 1
ISBN 13: 978-0-8229-6139-0
ISBN 10: 0-8229-6139-3

In Memory of

Mercedes Valdivieso (1924–1993)

and

Elizabeth Dietz (1964–2005)

For Orly Caroline Schoolman-Wood, the future

The concept of sin is tied up with this abstract, ultimate authority which we often call God. But I think there's also a sense of sin against yourself which is important to me and really means the same thing. Usually, it results from weakness, from the fact that we're too weak to resist temptation; the temptation to have more money, comfort, to possess a certain woman or man, or the temptation to hold more power.

Krzysztof Kieslowski

Contents

the

book

of

ten

The Lord God Returns

■

The day my friend died the ivory-billed woodpecker was maybe seen
in Arkansas, a bird long-thought extinct. Some say it's an image
of loss returned as an image of hope, but I don't know.
I'm not saying there was any correspondence,
just an interesting coincidence I noticed when loss seemed everywhere.
That was the same month a woman rescued a pair of red-billed ducks
and their fifteen ducklings from six lanes of Main Street
and herded them into a pond behind the Faculty Club.
Such odd birds that mate for life, the male and female
looking exactly alike. All that afternoon I watched them
in the pond, the father perched on the concrete edge
flapping his wings as if to warn us away, and the babies
circling and circling behind their mother in perfect formation,
always avoiding one small dead bird face down in the water.
There is grandeur in this view of life, Darwin wrote.
She was only forty. I don't think she believed in that
High Church Episcopal God her parents buried her by,
but I don't know what she believed exactly.
I believe the Lord God has returned to Arkansas, a bird
that got its name because our ancestors shouted "Lord God!"
whenever they saw it, a bird the size of a small child,
its jackhammer beak, a wingspan as long as a tall man's arm.
In 1837, when Audubon came here to Houston,
he saw ivory bills nesting up and down the banks of Buffalo Bayou.
Now it's all sludge and skyscrapers. In his famous painting,
the only place anyone has seen the bird for sixty years,
the male cocks his red head, seems to cast his beady, yellow eye
toward the painter as if to say, "Don't count me out!"
Of course, the birds were dead when Audubon painted them.

Later, all over the South, they flew out of the nineteenth century and
    disappeared
in time. But I like to think of my great-great-grandmother and her daughters
fleeing over the Ozarks, how they might have stopped
to rest their horses and heard an ivory bill *BAM-bamming*
in a tupelo tree, *kent-kenting* like a tin horn, and shouted "Lord God!"
when they looked up and saw it. Maybe they thought it was a sign
they were bound for better things when all they were bound for
was Texas, the poverty of a small town, its sharp gasps
and held breaths. Still, they were alive, the big house burned
behind them, the land burned, the husband and father,
the Welshman Cawthron, dead somewhere with the First Missouri—
Pea Ridge, Vicksburg, Nashville—gold plates and silver bridles
in the sacks of the carpetbaggers. Or that other ancestor,
my Cherokee great-great-great-grandmother, who wandered off the Trail of
    Tears
and onto a sharecropper's farm, her only possession a Cherokee Bible
she couldn't read. Maybe she stood in the dirt of that dirt-poor farm
and exclaimed "Lord God!" when her tow-headed husband
pointed to the woodpecker in the loblolly pine.
Did it remind her of the home she'd left behind, this bird
whose beak her tribe fashioned into coronets to crown its princesses?
Or maybe it was just a distraction in her ragtag life, the worry
of babies dying before they were two, of cotton crops gone up in drought.
She couldn't see me down the trail of years writing this poem
and maybe she wouldn't have cared if she could.
But I'm here, aren't I? At least for now. Don't count me out.
There is grandeur in this view of life.
Funny how we hunker down in our little canoes
in the middle of the scummy green swamp and wait and wait
for hope to appear, for ghosts to die and come back as bodies.

Decalogue: Thin Ice

■

When the boy finds a dead dog, he's sad
and wants to know why we die, what God is.
His aunt hugs him and tells him God
is here, in their embrace. Life,
she says, is a gift, though I'd have to say
sometimes it's a gag gift, like a huge flower
that squirts water at you when you put your nose
right up to it to smell it or the whoopee cushion
you sit on, unsuspectingly, in your favorite chair.
And maybe sometimes the joke turns cruel, so that
the boy's father calculates the strength
of the ice, but his math is wrong,
it won't hold up and the icy lake won't either,
won't hold up the boy and his flashing skates
just this once. It's too simple to say
the movie's director wants us to believe
the ice cracks and the boy dies to appease
some jealous Old Testament God
who's angry because the father worships science
instead of Him, or that he wants us to believe
the young man with the implacable stare, the one
who tends a fire on the lake shore,
is some kind of avenging angel. Maybe
he's God himself, impotent as anyone,
who looks on but can't change the world
he's set in motion. A philosopher might call what happens
the intrusion of the Meaningless Real. As a parent,
I'd call it The Thing You Must Not Name.
It's the break in the ice we all fear most and secretly
believe we deserve, that if God were just

he would rain down punishment on us
for all our little failures of attention,
for every time we were too tired, we were
too busy, every time we lost our tempers
and yelled, lost our tempers
and slapped. And not just any punishment,
but This One. We all have our little gods, of course—
the little god of self, for example, its ooze
and shine, its groan and moan—I've known
that kiss—and what of those of us whose sins
were huge, what of us, The Ones Who Left?
Nothing terrible happened. Pain, of course,
like anyone, but sometimes they grew up to be
productive, reasonably happy, while my friend,
who stayed married all those years, her son died
in a hit-and-run. Does that mean anything?
I don't think so. I suppose there might be
a certain comfort in believing in divine retribution—
at least you'd have a reason for why
things turned out the way they did. But I don't
believe in it any more than I believe in Providence, the kind
my father believes in, that God looks after him personally,
so that He made my father's car break down in front
of a gas station and not somewhere else. The way I see it,
they're both ways of feeling important. I mean,
that just leaves too many unanswered questions.
So every time something bad happens to you, are you
supposed to think it's because you were bad?
Or if it's good, is it because you were good? No,
I believe in meaningless coincidence—coincidence
that happens even to those who seem to live
in some dream of perfect happiness. Take this,
for instance: One summer night a young mother
bathes her children and puts them in the car and drives

to the airport to pick up her husband. They're a little late
because the younger girl couldn't find her "blankie" and so
they had to look everywhere, finally finding it
at the bottom of a basket of laundry, and maybe the mother
is impatient, scolds her daughter for still having to carry
the blanket with her everywhere so that the child cries,
sobbing in the backseat all the way to the airport.
When they arrive, her husband is already waiting
at the curb. It's been a long week in Boise,
and he's so happy to see them he doesn't care that
they're late and promises to stop for ice cream on the way home.
He's telling his wife what a jerk the client, Hopwagon, is
and the kids laugh about the name, and she's thinking how much
she missed him, how she can't wait to get the kids
to bed so they can make love, and just then,
as they round a curve on the overpass, a truck
traveling in the outside lane, the trucker
on his way home to see *his* wife and kids
in El Paso, maybe he's had a couple of beers,
maybe he's going a little too fast, or maybe
nothing at all, there's no reason,
he just loses control, and the semi, this huge tractor-trailer,
topples over onto the family's little station wagon,
which, of course, bursts into flames, but not before
someone pulls the mother to safety. Everyone else,
the father and three kids, are trapped, and the rescuers
have to hold onto her, she keeps trying to go back for them.
"They were screaming and there was nothing
we could do," the fireman said. "She kept saying
she didn't want to live." I couldn't imagine why
she would. Oh, and don't try to tell me
this is beyond our understanding, that it's all
part of God's plan, because the god who'd plan this,
he doesn't even deserve the name.

5

The Soul Bone

■

Once I said I didn't have a spiritual bone
in my body and meant by that
I didn't want to think of death,
as though any bone in us
could escape it. Maybe
I was afraid of what I couldn't know
for certain, a thud like the slamming
of a coffin lid, as final and inexplicable
as that. What was the soul anyway,
I wondered, but a homonym for loneliness?
Now, in late middle age, or more, I like to imagine it,
the spirit, the soul bone, as though it were hidden
somewhere inside my body, white as a tooth
that falls from a child's mouth, a dove,
the cloud it can fly through. Like bones,
it persists. Little knot of self, stubborn
as wildflowers in a Chilmark field in autumn,
the white ones they call boneset, for healing,
or the others, pearly everlasting.
The rabbis of the Midrash believed in the bone
and called it the *luz*, just like the Spanish word
for light, the size of a chickpea or an almond,
depending on which rabbi was telling the story,
found, they said, at the top of the spine or the base,
depending. No one's ever seen it, of course,
but sometimes at night I imagine I can feel it,
shining its light through my body, the bone
luminous, glowing in the dark. Sometimes,
if you listen, you might even hear that light
deep inside me, humming its brave little song.

Decalogue: What If

■

I want to tell her not to
do it, the sick man's wife who's pregnant

by her lover after she and her husband
have tried for years. She's trying

to decide: if her husband lives,
she'll have an abortion; if he dies,

she won't. And the lover
wants her too, of course, since this is

the softening light of the movies. She'll break his heart,
he says, but he knows she has to choose.

Another problem for an ethics class.
What would I do? What did I?

My problem wasn't so complicated, only
a man I didn't want, a man

who didn't want me, my own sad history
of motherhood. Still, sometimes I think

about her—I know it would've been
a girl, a second chance, the one

I'd never slap or turn away from, certainly
never leave. When she learned to read, she wouldn't

keep it from me because I'd wanted it so much,
wouldn't hide the plump-lipped vowels,

the bony consonants under her tongue
like forbidden candy. She wouldn't think I'd take

everything from her, the way my mother took
everything from me. She'd be turning

twenty-one this year, November, just now
when the Chinese tallow tree outside my door

shakes its gold curls. Spendthrift, it spills
its purse of gold coins on the ground.

Now she'd be bowing her own gold head
over the book of her life she'd just begun to write.

But I know it's sentimental
to think this way—to idealize the unknown—

when I made the only choice I could. I wouldn't
change it, not really. And it's foolish to think

I could've changed myself, become the maker of delicate
smocked dresses, shiner of patent leather shoes. I never told

the man, the father, who'd cried once, telling me how much
he wanted a child. Whatever happened to him?

And what about the woman who's trying to decide?
It's too late for her now, while sunlight elaborates

the scars on the lengthening day. Beside her husband's bed,
a jar of fruit she's left him, cherries perhaps.

Over this vast sea of fruit, a wasp struggles
up the silver pole of a spoon. It slips

and falls, then pulls itself back on the spoon
like someone scrambling for a lifeboat. This happens

again and again, until I almost give up hope.
Finally, it reaches the rim of the glass, pauses and looks

around, compound eyes taking in the broken world.
Then it shakes the bloodred fruit from its wings and flies away.

Soledad

∎

In Piazzolla's tangos, it's always Buenos Aires,
1950 something, a dim cafe—the Richmónd de Florida, perhaps.
All the men are smoking, drinking small white cups
of thick, black coffee, while Piazzolla, master of the bandoneon,
plays a tango *a la parilla*, freely, without a score
(a phrase that also signifies "the way meat is grilled just long enough
to seal it on both sides"). Improvisation is like grief,
you never know when it will take you by surprise.

It's the way he never knows when he'll turn a corner near the Recoleta
and see his beloved walking away down an empty street and the melody
is the pure song of pain. Piazzolla will be young only a little longer.
His black hair, just beginning to recede to silver at the temples,
is slicked back in the manner of the day, and his eyes, too, shine
black and wet, like a pond without moonlight, though whether they fill
with rain or memories, no one can say.

It is December, summer, hot and sweet, and he is sweating now,
a thin film like milk on his upper lip. He imagines a woman—
he'll call her Mercedes—floating near the ceiling like an angel
in a painting by Chagall, except she's no angel and the clouds
she floats above are smoke. She had no mercy,
raking her red nails across his back when she came,
moaning his name, "Astor! Astor!" He remembers that.

He knows it's a scene predictable as a telenovela, but still
he can't forget it, can't forget how her body felt
beneath him in that room, the fan making its useless circles
in the stifling air, the same motion his finger made tracing

the lilac areolas of her nipples. He'd go back there if he could.
But most of all he longs to postpone the moment of release,
to make it go on and on the way grief can,
the way in "Soledad" he postpones the resolution
of harmonic sequences until I think my heart will break.

It's as though I've found at last a house I dreamed of once,
found it down the side street of a dream of Buenos Aires,
a place I've never been. Still, I know the house is mine and I find it
there, find it behind a wall of brick and jacaranda,
but when I open the iron gate I see it's deserted now,
Perón has taken everyone away and no one knows me anymore.
Inside the dusty rooms, I can still hear his song, a phonograph
playing it over and over in the empty air. *Soledad.*

Decalogue: Rooms

■

I've been lonely like that, that woman skidding
through icy, deserted streets, crashing
into small, lighted trees that litter the vacant lots.

She's always behind glass looking out or outside
looking in where it's always Christmas Eve
and a lamplit family lifts flutes

of champagne. She always has one white pill
in her pocket she's keeping in reserve.
She's chosen this, of course, nursing despair

the way someone else might lean on a bar nursing
a single malt Scotch, something peaty and strong.
She'll do anything to make you love her.

I've been like her. In various cities I walked
through leafy neighborhoods, dusk spreading
out its blue tablecloth, hanging its curtain of pale stars

in the sky, and peered in vinegar-cleaned windows
where families posed before fireplaces,
a tableau vivant, their arms draped casually on mantels.

Envy tugged at my sleeve, kept dragging me back
to look. Afterwards, I huddled in the corner
of my body as though that body were a locked room

someone might break into at any moment.
I was alone there, so alone it was like drowning,
and I could hear birds outside crying in the bois d'arc trees,

their sounds reaching me as from a great distance,
the phoebe's *pit-tee, pit-tee*, the kestrel's *killy, killy*,
so that for years I thought such loneliness was air.

I Got a Mind to Ramble

■

Alberta Hunter at The Cookery, 1981

Winter, deep dark, the Village streets deserted, so cold even the
    homeless
have disappeared, and my friend and I are walking to The Cookery,
University Place and Eighth Street, both of us recently divorced
and so much alike—literary, smart, neurotic, a little narcissistic—

that her ex-husband keeps asking me out, but I don't want to trade
my old unhappy life for its identical twin. The air icy with our talk,
those nights examining our marriages over and over, like Darwin
examining his earthworms, except the men are always the worms

and we're the survival of the fittest, first ones off
the sinking ship of marriage. It'll take years
to admit our own worminess. Oh, we're shameless,
wearing our heavy coats of sadness, our guilt-tight gloves

like decorations. All we want is transformation—
I got a mind to ramble, but I don't know where to go—
the tropics, bikinis and Ban de Soleil, piña coladas
at the swim-up bar, and long-lashed pool boys leering

from the cabanas. I'm in love with someone else, someone
who isn't in love with me, and I don't want to be.
At fourteen Susan Sontag had a crush on Thomas Mann
while I had a crush on Ray Weems, the quarterback, so what hope

is there for me at thirty-four in love with the grownup equivalent
of a football hero? At least we have the good grace to be sick
of ourselves, a little bit anyway. Inside The Cookery, the air's
heavy with smoke, steam heat, the crowd hushed

and expectant, and then the spotlight comes up and there she is,
a tiny woman filling the room, bangle earrings almost as big as her head
—poor Memphis black child, Chicago potato peeler, star, then nurse,
then star again, the latest sensation at eighty-five. To sing the blues

is not to have the blues, which are, after all, less about sadness
than triumph and revenge, and she doesn't,
this high-yellow gal with the Indian nose, though she knows
we think she's a cutie pie, Miss Thing, and she's playing us,

jiving, the way she teases "I Got a Mind to Ramble," slapping
her hip like a tambourine, the dark, rich voice now a wink, now
a growl, a voice someone called "a contralto that wears boots."
"Ladies," she says, dispensing advice between songs,

"if you tell a man you love him, you're in a bad fix.
He's gonna ruin you. Don't let that happen to you, honey."
And then she segues into "Down Hearted Blues," a song
she wrote in 1922, fingers snapping, eyes rolling—

Gee, but it's hard to love someone,
when that someone don't love you.
I'm so disgusted, heartbroken too.
I've got the downhearted blues. . . .

I've got the world in a jug and the stopper in my hand.
I've got the world in a jug and the stopper in my hand.
And if you want me, pretty papa, you've got to come under my command.

And aren't we transformed for a moment?
For an evening we believe her, or believe we do,
women who don't need men, who don't need love, the world
and everything in it for once at our command.

What did we know? Not much. Surely not how long it takes,
the slow, blind ramble toward change, to arrive, if ever, at something
provisional as wisdom. I wonder now if she saw, when she looked out
into that dark night of white faces, how lost we were on the starless road,

how alone and thirsty, no jug, no stopper anywhere in sight.
And maybe she might even have pitied us a little, this old woman
who'd spent one of her lifetimes mastering a kind of Braille,
emptying the bedpans of the dying, thumbing shut the dumb eyes of the
    dead.

Decalogue: Husbands and Wives

■

Because Kieslowski's subject is the enduring power of love,
of course when Roman discovers his impotency is permanent and suggests
to Hanka that she divorce him, she says no, insists love
is in the heart and not between the legs. She does, in fact, take a lover,
a young man with hair the color of the pale Polish sun, but of course
he doesn't fulfill her. She feels guilty and sends him away,
the way one might banish a naughty child picking flowers in one's garden:
"Do up your jacket and be off." Of course
Roman discovers her betrayal and wants to die, riding

his little bicycle off a cliff, its wheels spinning back and forth,
like the legs of a cartoon character, say Wile E. Coyote,
trying to stop himself in midair.
Of course he doesn't die. Of course
when he calls Hanka from the hospital, the telephone
in their apartment just rings and rings
because Hanka's afraid to answer. Of course
she picks it up weeping, whispers, "God, are you there?"
meaning, maybe, not just Roman, but God Himself.

And all this from a director so famously morose
he never smiles in his photographs, just stands there
looking down with his hangdog beard, his doggy eyes, a man
of whom his friend Adam, who is also my friend, said,
"He vas very gloomy"—I can't get the accent right,
but it was said with all the Eastern European dolor he could muster—
a man who was the subject of a film called *I'm So-So,*
his natural state, a man so notoriously stubborn he refused to go
to Paris where all the good heart surgeons were, despite the fact

that he could afford it and everyone urged him to go, but instead
he insisted on staying in Warsaw to have the operation
at some crumbling, post-Soviet hospital. Of course he died.
I suppose if even he could believe in the redemptive power of love,
I can too—oh, I've seen it in my own life, in the love of family and friends,
in the few couples I know whose intimacy seems to go on and on
like birdsong in the trees this afternoon, despite all the many annoyances,
the way even birdsong itself can be annoying. Sometimes it shrills
like the rasping of the workmen's saws at the house across the field.

I'm feeling so-so myself today—not just the saws or the pain
in my tailbone where I slipped on the wet steps this morning,
but of course more lies from the president, of course more genocide
in Darfur, of course thirty-four children waiting for American soldiers
to hand out candy were killed by a car bomb in Baghdad and a mother
holds up a bleeding child whose open mouth seems to be forming
some version of "Mama! Mama!" which of course sounds to me
like "Nada! Nada!" I'm so-so in spite of that one white flower
blooming in the garden, some kind of lily, its petals resembling

the feathers of a bird, a dove, maybe, so-so despite the afternoon sun
tatting its lace in intricate patterns all over the lawn. Maybe
I am thinking of my own marriage, which is petty of me
in the face of all the bad news in the world, but there it is,
my marriage, with its failures of love and nerve, its bad omens
from the start—the wedding day on which I hid
in my mother's closet among the winter suits and wept
and tried to tell myself it was just wedding-day jitters
though I knew it wasn't, not to mention the wedding ring

I put on his right hand instead of his left, the album
of wedding pictures lost in our first move. But that doesn't explain

anything, really. Every unhappy marriage is unhappy in its own way,
I suppose, but sometimes it's the impossible ideal that strands you
there with the knife in your hand or the words "I never loved you"
curling on your lips, the way my ex was stranded in sadness
every Sunday. Fridays, the blue Pacific's still to be crossed,
green island of Saturday looming ahead, a Hawaii of leis
and piña coladas at the swim-up bar in a pool beside the sea,

but by Sunday rain has kept them in all weekend,
the paper soggy on the front walk, bills to pay and children
bored in the TV's blue light, his wife locked in her study
dreaming of someone else. Oh, it was always the same:
we were never who the other thought we were.
And I remember being afraid of him, the rage that broke down
the study door, threw a coffee cup against the wall, though, really, I feared
my own rage as much as his. Once he swerved on an icy road, back and
        forth,
threatening to shove me out into the dark. Hadn't I provoked him, though?

The man I loved, who didn't love me, whose voice on the phone
made my husband throw the coffee cup, told me he wanted to put his hands
inside a woman's body and wrap them around her heart,
as though it were a gift wrapped up in shiny red paper, a gift
just for him. I knew the heart he wanted wasn't mine, but still
I walked with him at night, the yellow coin of moon pressed
against the dark eyes of the field, his words pressing into me like stars
in the river we walked beside. I knew I was alone, but still,
for years I courted that loss, the sheer impossibility of it.

We never slept together, though my husband never believed me.
The man wasn't the reason I wanted to leave.
Still, sometimes I dream I'm back in that marriage and know

this time I'll have to stay. Sometimes I even like it.
But if my husband had threatened back then to die if I left,
would I have stayed? I think you know the answer.
If Hanka was faithful in her heart but unfaithful in her body,
then I was faithful in my body but unfaithful in my heart.
Tell me, which is worse?

Custody

∎

The dog dragged it out from under the refrigerator, the dead mouse,
a perfect specimen of a mouse, so like a cartoon mouse it didn't seem real,
like Jerry who made life miserable for Tom the Cat
on Saturday morning TV, this one so recently dead it wasn't even stiff,
making my dog miserable too, because it wouldn't move when he nudged it
with his cold nose, because I had to tie him up before I could scoop it up
and carry it outside to the trash bin. The next day
when I went back to look I found it gone, simply vanished
as if it had never been. Had some predator carried it off or had its brothers
come to bear it away for a proper mouse funeral,
one acting the priest, one the gravedigger? Maybe it hadn't been
dead at all, just playing possum—playing dead mouse?—and had simply
        risen up
and scampered away. Somehow I wanted that to be the case
despite its filth, the dirt and droppings, the harm it can do in a house,
the way a whole continent once wanted Jesse James to be still alive,
        disguised
as some poor farmer in the West, or D. B. Cooper to survive jumping from
        the plane,
the way we sometimes can't help rooting for the murderer on TV
to outwit the smart cop after all, want our baser natures to triumph
just this once. But today there was another mouse, this one
sitting still in the middle of the kitchen floor, and because by now
I was tired of mice, I went after it with the broom,
though I could see it was dying already, had probably eaten poison
under the house, and though it wanted to live still,
like every living thing, its tiny feet scrabbling to stay upright,
I swept it out onto the deck and down onto the ground below,
where it lay still, dead then or soon to be.

"Custody of the eyes," the Polish nuns called it years ago
when my friend entered the convent, thirteen, a child. They meant by that
to cover oneself in a wimple of reflection, looking only inward
on the spirit, eyes downcast on the stone floor, never seeing
the others who passed in the hall those long, silent days. She left
when she came to believe there was more to see, the body itself,
for example, body of the lover spread open on the sunlit sheets, bodies
of the dead spilling their secrets in the anatomy lab—this was the world
she chose. Still, it's custody of that inner eye, the one looking
inward on the spirit, I find myself thinking of, the one
that sees me for what I am: someone who wanted one mouse to live
and the other to die, wanted it for no good reason except that I did,
the killer who wielded the broom like a golf club just because I could,
who smacked the little dying body and sent it flying to land *splat!*
like a cartoon mouse on the hard ground, someone
who now leans heavily on the broomstick, a little breathless
with my power, gloating even, in the unseasonably warm October air.

In America

■

Late afternoon, late February in San Diego, the sky a gauze bandage
     of blue light, the air
mild, springlike, and the young black man and I wait for the train
     at Seaport Village, just the two of us,
no seaport, no village in sight, just a place for tourists on their way
     to other tourist stops, Gas Lamp Quarter
or Old Town, other faux streets of restaurants and galleries,

of T-shirt shops and ye olde lampposts contrived for our distraction
     in the Year of Our Lord 2002.
He looks harmless enough in his clean, faded shirt and baggy jeans,
     his body soft, doughy,
as though if I touched him my thumbprint would stay visible
     on his flesh forever.
I have friends who know what it is to have a woman

cross to the other side of the street, to be pulled over by cops for no reason—
     DWB, they call it, Driving While Black—
but I can't help it, when he asks for a dollar for the train, something deep
     in my body turns over,
flops like a hooked fish on a line. He's all dimples and baby fat,
     but still, when he opens
the brown paper sack, I imagine a gun in there, a gun black

and thick as his arm, but then I see what he has wrapped up
     in a shiny red box.
He's on his way to the mall in El Cajon where his girlfriend works
     nights at Smoothie King, and tonight
he's going to ask her to marry him, he's finally going to do it.

He points to the Band-Aid
on his arm and tells me he sold his blood to pay for the ring

even though he's terrified of needles. First thing next week he's going
        to enlist in the Army
if he can pass the test this time. He'll have to lose weight, he says,
        but he can do it, and if they get married
now, she can have his benefits. You can see the stars in his eyes,
        gold flecks in the deep brown
that shine in the night sky of his face. In two minutes, I've gone from fear

for *my* life to fear for *his* life, and I'm relieved when the train arrives at last
        because I don't know what to say
about his dreams, which I believe will come to nothing, because this is
    America,
        where the poor stay poor and hope
is not, as Emily Dickinson said, *a thing with feathers*, but is, as someone
        once said of the comb-over,
an acceptable convention that doesn't really fool anybody.

Two stops later I'm off with a quick "Good luck"—it's a pleasantry
        that seems too little and not right.
He smiles and waves, holds up the ring box for me to see one last time,
        and is gone down the tracks.
For months afterward I can't stop wondering what happened to him,
        if he got married, joined the Army.
Maybe he got sent to Iraq. Maybe he died there.

I watch the news every night, thinking I might see him somewhere
        among the soldiers in the burning streets.
Of course, I've forgotten exactly what he looked like, though I keep trying
        to recall his face, his face like the dark side
of the moon pressed against the window of the swiftly moving train.

After His Retirement, LBJ Visits Greenville

■

It must've been nineteen seventy or seventy-one—
both Kennedys dead, Dr. King dead, the war
that drove Johnson from the White House seeming as if
it will never end, a few boys from home burned up
in the faraway jungle, the boy who sat beside me
in algebra class, who came back alive, dead
when his drug-smuggling plane crashed somewhere
along the Mexican border. Now Nixon is President,
we don't know about Watergate yet and the Democrats
have little hope, but we go anyway, a fundraiser
for some long forgotten congressman, summer, hot, the sun
a boil on the concrete skin of the parking lot. Greenville, Texas.
Inside the Holiday Inn's small reception room,
it's hotter still, but no one wants to leave.
Over the sweaty handshakes, the *Howdies* and back slaps,
a rumor floats: LBJ himself is coming.
So we stay on, stay on for the bad wine, the bad hors d'oeuvres—
triangle sandwiches of tuna fish, celery stuffed with pimento cheese—
stay on while the light outside dwindles to dark,
curious to see this man who already seems almost apocryphal.
Years before, running against Kennedy, he'd helicoptered
to our little town—we'd never seen a helicopter!—
and at the high school an auditorium full of kids waiting, rapt.
I can't imagine why he came there—we couldn't even vote—
but there he was, as they say down here, big as Texas.
When he draped his long form over the podium and drawled,
"Y'all tell your mommies and daddies that ol' Lyndon says Howdy!"
the whole room erupted with our claps and cheers, all of us,
even those who'd sneered at him before, lifted

in those long arms, believing we had seen the future,
he seemed so much one of us. In a week or two a few of us,
in secret, would be back in love with JFK, a Yankee
but so handsome, the same ones who'd someday be
marching in the streets, a whole generation screaming,
Hey, hey, LBJ, how many boys did you kill today?
We were only children. Now some of us have children
of our own to put to bed, jobs to go to in the morning, the rumor
of his coming like a fable that foretells the coming of a stranger.
But when I turn to go, opening the door,
he's standing there on the other side, not reaching
for the doorknob, just standing there, his huge body
filling the frame, but changed, older, the hound-dog eyes
and hound-dog face cast down, somehow more naked
than when he showed his scars on television, abashed even,
a young boy screwing up his courage to knock on his first date's door.
Then he looks up, and in the moment before he catches himself
and grins that big grin, sticks out his hand, I see he knows
he's already dead, his eyes the vast plains of West Texas
where you could drive and drive for hours
and never see another living soul.

"The Strange Case of the Virgin Lidwina"

■

First recorded case of multiple sclerosis, 1421

In the drawing she looks a little like photographs
of both my grandmother and me, same long face,
heavy eyelids, and maybe if I could trace my family
back to fourteenth-century Holland, I'd find an ancestor,
some still unknown gene passed on to me
these six hundred years. Back then she was just another
Dutch teenager, centuries before the term was invented,
out skating with her friends. Delft blue sky,
the hard sun cracking open the afternoon.
She'd been showing off, as she liked to do,
always the best skater, blades forming
the edges of a perfect figure 8. Just an ordinary
winter day in Schiedam, a girl floating free
in the wind. And then she wasn't. Facedown
on the ice, she heard the voices of her friends
as if from far away, calling, "Lidwy, Lidwy, get up!"
And couldn't. Soon, paralyzed, nearly blind,
her face twitching in pain, she had little to do
but think. When the doctor said her illness
came from God and couldn't be cured,
she decided to make the most of it and declared
she'd been called to suffer for the sins of others.
Suffering would be her joy now. Who could resist such
sympathy, even pity, especially when it's all you have?
Who doesn't like to be the center of attention?
Pretty soon the villagers flocked to press their noses
against the windows of the sick room, worshipping.
Thirty-seven years she lay there in that hushed room,
while legends sprang up around her like roses
on the wall outside her window. That her twisted body

gave off the fragrance of those roses,
that her dark room glowed with such holy light
the peasants thought it must be on fire.
In later years it was said she took no nourishment
but Christ's blood and body. I wonder if she'd think
it was all worth it now to know she's the patron saint
of figure skaters, all those healthy Tanyas and Taras
and Sashas and Michelles set spinning in homage.
I wonder if she'd think how much the world has changed
or how little, these days when some see the image
of the Virgin Mary on a pie pan, the face of Jesus
in a corn tortilla, these days when a machine lights up
my brain so the lesions seem to float there, white
as the Milky Way, dark as a black hole.

A Short History of Women in the Nineteenth Century
■

In the Mütter Museum, Dr. Hyrtl's skulls in a glass case,
    laid out along the shelves like so much fine porcelain.

If they could talk to us, they'd say, *What are you staring at?*
    Don't you know you're going to end up just like us?

Just wait and see if you don't. At night, though, in the dark,
    they talk to each other, the women

telling their stories over and over, like stitches ripped out
    and resewn. As usual, the men are silent,

except for a few rough words. *Hold your tongue, woman!*
    Can't you ever give a fellow a moment's peace?

But the women won't listen. This time they won't stop speaking.
    Francesca Seycora, age nineteen, famous prostitute,

dead of meningitis. *Oh, I was a fine lady, I was,*
    silk skirts dragging Vienna's gutters.

I remember this boy, Sigmund, I used to talk to
    on his way to school. A pretty child.

He asked me why I was a bad woman. His mother,
    that hausfrau, had told him I was a whore.

Because I like to eat, I said. A swelling in the brain
    got me before some swell did.

Then there's the Slovenian, Magdal Payzac, a maid dead
    at twenty-three of childbed fever. *No wonder,*

dirt everywhere, shit in the streets. It was the master's child,
    I was better off dead. The baby died too.

In Salzburg, Veronica Huber, eighteen, executed
    for murdering hers. *What was I going to do*

with a baby? You tell me that. Me,
    with no husband, no work. God

spoke to me, I put a pillow over her head until
    she stopped crying. I wasn't sorry.

Another, nameless, ageless, dying alone in Amsterdam,
    a suicide. *When he left me, I didn't know*

what to do. I didn't want to live anymore, so I jumped
    into the canal, stones in my pockets.

Across the room, all alone on another shelf, the American, Ellen Jones,
    calls out to them: *You think you had it bad—*

just look at me. See this big piece of pie gone
    from my skull. George Wilkinson was drunk,

went after me with an axe. I let him climb on top of me
    any time he wanted, but when he touched

my daughter, I said I was leaving. I didn't care
    what happened to us, just not that.

When he picked up the axe, I told her to run. Run fast,
  I said. At the trial, even with his bloody clothes,

they let him off. No one would believe a seven-year-old girl.
  I tell you, these people passing here every day,

all of them exclaiming over my poor, hurt head, these people,
  I swear, they just don't know anything yet.

Daily Life

∎

A parrot of irritation sits
on my shoulder, pecks
at my head, ruffling his feathers
in my ear. He repeats
everything I say, like a child
trying to irritate the parent.
Too much to do today: the dracena
that's outgrown its pot, a mountain
of bills to pay and nothing in the house
to eat. Too many clothes need washing
and the dog needs his shots.
It just goes on and on, I say
to myself, no one around, and catch
myself saying it, a ball hit so straight
to your glove you'd have to be
blind not to catch it. And of course
I hope it does go on and on
forever, the little pain,
the little pleasure, the sun
a blood orange in the sky, the sky
parrot blue and the day
unfolding like a bird slowly
spreading its wings, though I know,
saying it, that it won't.

If Grief Were a Bird

■

Last night I woke up in the still dark and the cold
to the sounds of the birds starting up in the trees
just before dawn, some old, half-remembered sadness
hovering over me, flapping its wings, and I wondered
if grief were a bird, what would it be?
Maybe an African Gray, an annoying bird
that won't shut up, just talks and talks and says the same thing over
and over, the way the griever keeps saying the beloved's name
again and again, saying it and weeping and can't stop. And then
there are the sounds that bird makes, exact imitations
of the sounds we hear every day, domestic sounds, the sounds
we take for granted, and the bird's imitations are enough
to drive you crazy, sending you running back and forth
all over the house. First, it's the doorbell, but when you open
the door, no one is there, no one is ever there. Then
the phone rings and rings and you answer, but the line
is dead, and the microwave buzzes, but there's nothing
inside, the oven is empty. All this until you're so exhausted
you crave oblivion, oblivion of drink, oblivion of sleep,
oblivion the black cloth like the one that covers the bird's cage.
Or maybe if grief were a bird, it would be a vicious bird, a vulture
that waits by the highway, red meat of your heart
spilled on the road, your heart's meat its food, what it needs
to live. It wants to kill you, it pecks and pecks
and can never get enough, the way the griever feels
that pain, the heart torn away bit by bit, and the body, the body
picked clean to the bone, but still the pain never ends, that phantom pain.
Or maybe if grief were a bird, it would be one you could tame,

but not completely. Maybe it would follow you
everywhere and sit on your shoulder, preening and grooming itself,
a bright yellow cockatiel. You scratch its head, it nuzzles your neck.
You feed it bread from your hand, it's grateful, it loves you. But sometimes
it bites—not enough bread, or you haven't been paying it enough attention,
it wants you to notice, it bites till you bleed. Sometimes it's sleeping,
it's quiet, so quiet you forget for a long time that it's there,
sleeping in its cage. You love the bird then,
you've been together so long, it's your companion, your friend.
You know it will never leave you. Sometimes you even think it *is* you:
you look into its black, beady eyes and see yourself
staring back, shrieking that lost name.

My Father Looks Down on Me

■

He says he's up there on the ledge and points
toward the ceiling where the TV
is soldered to the wall, but the TV's
on the floor, he says, and the table
pulled across his hospital bed tilts
like the Alps so that everything—
pitcher, glass, box of Kleenex—will slide off
if I don't catch it. Of course,
he wants me to catch him too,
but I don't understand and keep
insisting he's *not* on the ledge,
the TV's *not* on the floor, and he
just gets madder and madder, the sound
of anger from my childhood, wasps
buzzing and whirring, a sound that builds
and builds until they're outside the nest swirling
around my head like a fierce, black cloud and I
have nowhere to run, not like the anger that hides
inside, a naughty child afraid to come out
and be punished. "I'm not stupid!" my father shouts—
he always says that, he thinks I think that.
I keep telling him I don't.
He's ninety now, and looks it, finally—chicken neck,
mouth open when he sleeps so that he looks dead
and I have to stare hard every time
I come into the room to see if he's breathing.
Sometimes I think he'll never die, that maybe
he's immortal. It's true that all his life

he's played by the rules, such a good boy
he wouldn't even change seats with me
on the airplane, even though he wanted to
sit on the aisle because—as he'll tell anyone—
he has a "prostrate" problem—he couldn't move,
he said, because the airline had him
on the list as 8B so he had to stay there.
I tried to tell him no one cared, that people change
all the time, but he just looked at me
with that stubborn, no-point-arguing face
like there's a frozen tundra inside him. I think
he's just furious because he's played by these rules
and what is he supposed to do now, when there's only
one rule and that's death? He's scared of dying.
Sometimes he weeps and says he's had a good life,
that God will take care of him—personally,
he means, like the time he said God made his car
break down in front of a gas station
rather than late at night on some lonely road.
It seems like if you believed that, you wouldn't
be afraid of dying. And then I remember
what the nurse said. "It's the anesthesia,"
I tell him. "That's what's making you see things
like that, making you think you're up there
on the ledge." But he just looks at me,
a sullen, swelled-up glare, like *I'm* the parent,
his parent, about to send him out again
to find his father's whiskey bottles
hidden in the barn. All my life
I've known that look, it's even tucked away
in the family Bible, in sepia, circa 1919.
It must've been a special occasion,

his birthday, maybe. Against a backdrop of palms,
he's six, dressed as a WWI doughboy, small arms
closed like a barricade across the mine field of his body.
His eyes are flinty slits, his lower lip's
a precipice. He should just jump.

Benediction

∎

Nights and weekends he'd close himself up
in the bedroom, a boy in his clubhouse,

watching baseball or football, whatever sport
was in season, old westerns, sitcoms, the only place

he could get away from his anger, I guess,
a rage I seemed to stoke each night at dinner

with my incessant talking, my smart mouth,
his face a furnace, smoke bellowing from his lips.

Did I remind him too much of lack,
of helplessness, the childhood he didn't want

to visit? He stayed up there so much
my grandmother thought he must be a drunk

like his father, like his brother, but he never touched
the stuff. Candy was his drug for pain.

Some Sunday afternoons greed won over fear,
and I'd go up and he'd open for me

the sacks of sweets, Kraft caramels,
each one in its own wrapper

like a Christmas gift, or orange slices,
half-moons with their sprinkles of sugar stars.

I'd go up for candy and for what happened after,
the moment he'd take my legs and hold them

to the bed, tickling the bottoms of my feet
until I screamed for him to stop. And then

I'd beg for more and it would start
all over again until I'd begin to cry.

What he called "bearding" was the benediction,
a kind of hymn in praise of the father.

He'd hold me tight and scrape his unshaven cheek
against my own small, soft one, leaving it

red and stinging like bees. It hurt,
but it felt like love, so it must have been.

Decalogue: Fathers and Daughters

■

In a movie everything can be tidy as a small apartment in Warsaw,
the one where a father and his teenage daughter live together happily,
so happily in fact she thinks she's in love with him and forges
a letter from her long-dead mother saying he's not really

her father. They should just do it, she says, taking off
her shirt, showing him her girlish breasts, the tight,
pink areolas of the nipples, and the audience can see
the hunger in his eyes, and the sadness too, how he wants

to bury his face there before he covers her with a shirt,
refuses to break the Commandment. And of course,
she'll come clean eventually, admit she made the whole thing up.
But I kept thinking about Lot and his daughters,

a story in the Bible that used to fill me
with unease. In the distance Sodom burns,
and in the cave the old man's drunk, passed out,
his wife having conveniently turned into a pillar of salt,

while his daughters, believing he's the last man left
on earth, take their turns having sex with him. I wondered
if it was really to ensure the race or to shame him
for what he'd done in Sodom—hidden the angels from the mob

and offered instead the daughters? *Behold now,*
I have two daughters which have not known man;
let me, I pray you, bring them out unto you,
and do ye to them as is good in your eyes: only

unto these men do nothing. . . . The story has its own kind
of tidiness, I suppose, but it left me confused the way
my own father left me confused. By day he sat silently
in his armchair, only to rise to the kitchen table

where he shoveled a forkful of words back into his mouth
like a film rewound and my mother wept at the sink.
I pretended I was somewhere else and stared up
at the silly wallpaper where deer in wedding veils leapt

in rows endless as trees. It seemed so sad to be trapped
there in the snowy forest without their grooms.
Would I ever be a bride? Later, sent up to bed,
I felt the dark reach out its bony fingers and I was afraid

it would creep inside, the door to my body unlatched.
When I cried, why didn't my mother come?
Instead, my father lay down as if to comfort me,
but there was no comfort in the way we lay on opposite sides

of the bed as if we meant to keep a boat from tipping over,
no comfort in the way we lay, not like spoons, but knives,
turning our backs on each other. I didn't know what it meant,
that not-touching, but I knew enough to be ashamed.

No Commandment was broken, but sometimes I couldn't sleep.
Instead of counting sheep, I counted the deer, those brides
lost in the cold without their mates. In what world could they come
down from the wall and lie by the warm stove?

Palace Theater

∎

Those years before television, the first movie
I saw there—it was *Cinderella*—sent me screaming
up the aisle, the huge mice with their sharp teeth

looming over me, my mother chasing after me.
Later, I learned to love what I'd feared.
The dark more real than daylight, even

the scariest ones—*The Creature From the Black Lagoon*,
Them—that made me hide my eyes and crouch
under the torn leather seats. It wasn't much

of a palace, those ripped seats, the floor sticky
with spilled sodas, its faintly urinous odor, but in the dark
Doris Day whispered to Rock Hudson

on a Princess phone, her voice breathy with secrets,
and Grace Kelly and Cary Grant careened in a little car
down a steep hill, a place called the French Riviera

behind them, so fake it looked real. In the dark
every road was a road out of there.
I don't remember what the movie was

that day, it could've been anything. Nothing
was real but her father waiting for us in the dark
of the Palace Theater after school.

The red stitching on his shirt said "August," his name.
He smelled of gasoline. Outside it was May.
I was eight. He sat between us, put my hand

in his lap, something slick and soft as a mouse.
I didn't move. I'd been taught to obey the parent,
especially the father, to move softly

around his anger or else he wouldn't come
at night to save me when the dark pressed in
and the bad man hid underneath my bed.

Once I had read in a newspaper at breakfast
at the kitchen table—I was a precocious reader—
a story that said a girl was raped. I asked my mother

what that meant, to be raped, but I pronounced it wrong,
pronounced it as though it were *wrapped*, like a present,
or *rapt*, like awe. I don't remember her explanation.

I wasn't sure if this was the same thing,
but later, at home, I was sick. Sitting on the toilet
I told my mother what had happened, begged her

not to tell anyone, especially my father.
I don't remember what she said, if she said,
It wasn't your fault, you didn't do anything

wrong, said, He shouldn't have done that.
We never spoke of it again.
Years later, after she was dead, after

the Palace Theater had long been torn down,
I asked my father if she'd told him.
Yes, he said, she told me.

I asked him why they didn't do something.
She told me you didn't want us to, he said.
So they obeyed. As if I were the parent.

Dotage

■

Thirteen, fourteen, I'm still afraid
of the dark so the light from the bathroom
cuts a splinter of moon down the hall
the night my mother stumbles past the open door
of my room, her pink nylon nightgown
wadded at her hips. I see that
thousand-yard stare. Thirteen, fourteen,
I know what sex is, in theory
anyway. I know it hurts. I'm glass,
I'm willing myself to become shatterproof.
Years later, before she died, she told me
what she'd hated about sex, that he always
wanted a blow job. Of course, she didn't
say "blow job," she said something like
"he wanted me to put it in my mouth."
And I could imagine him, the heavy weight
of him, the wall, the will, the way
he always insists, insists, insists. I could
imagine him pressing the nape of her neck,
holding her head against him until
he shuddered into her, her fire-engine red lips
staining the shaft. The way now, ninety-three—
he can't wipe his own ass, can't wash
his own cock—he screams over and over
at the night nurse and calls her
a goddamned bitch, screams all night
and rattles the bars of the hospital bed
we put in his bedroom, demands she go

to the bank, go right now, no matter
it's 3 a.m., go to the bank and get the deeds
out of his lockbox because doesn't she know
someone is trying to steal his property?

Decalogue: Mothers and Daughters
■

Late September and the sun
slouches against the house, like a woman
with her hat in her hand, one hooded eye
slightly open. I'm gazing out
at the beech, that huge tree, maybe
the oldest tree on the Vineyard. If the neighbor
would just cut away the other trees, the pin oaks,

that have grown up around it,
I could see it plain, its big arms
spread over the still-green earth.
He doesn't want to kill any living thing,
he says. I am thinking of my mother,
whom I can't see plain either
for all the tangled underbrush in my mind.

In Kieslowski's film, the one
about mothers and daughters, the mother, horrified
by her pregnant daughter, raises her daughter's bastard
child as her own, but the daughter wants the child
back and tries to steal her. As always,
it's too late: the girl loves her grandmother best.
What is it that makes it so hard for us,

mothers and daughters, makes these forests
of love and rage so impossible to hack through?
Maybe it's our sameness, the girl child's body
so like the mother's we can't see
where one ends and the other begins.

In the film we don't know why
Eva seems not to love her daughter, Majka.

Is it something in her we can't know,
jealousy of Majka's youth, maybe, or something
in the daughter, who is, after all, sullen and resentful?
I'm smoking an illicit cigarette and remembering
how my mother's lungs turned to ashes,
to paper, and she grew so light, so light
she simply rose and floated away. Her love

was like that too, smothering, choking, inside it
the deep red of poppies like the air
back home in Houston on those hot days
when the fields in Mexico are being burned
and the smoke drifts north and you can taste it
on your tongue, feel it seeping deep into your body.
Here is the worst thing she ever said to me:

I know you better than you know yourself.
She was trying to convince me
not to marry the boy who asked.
It's true I haven't been married to him
for twenty years and she's been dead fifteen,
but still I can't forget it. Did I hate it
so much, hate her, because I knew

it wasn't true or because I was afraid it was?
Oh, I know she thought I only pretended
my chief emotion was despair. She called me
"Sarah Bernhardt," put her hand
to her forehead and staggered around the living room,

wailing. "That's you," she said.
She never knew I stole her silver hat pins,

never knew that late at night, locked in my room,
I played a game of Mother May I, undressing
the Little Women dolls one by one, jabbing
the pins again and again into the soft place
between their legs, pretending they were knives.
I saved the Marmee doll, the mother, for last,
for best. She hated the body, my mother,

the body with all its seepages and stinks,
its desire. If I loved despair,
it was because I had a good teacher, little girl
orphaned at five, and the only story
she ever told about those years was the one
where she overheard the aunts say,
"She's not p-r-e-t-t-y but she's s-m-a-r-t."

They thought she couldn't spell.
She always told me I was smart, and I thought
she wanted to steal my daughter too, a child
both pretty and smart, who at two ran headlong
into the edge of a door frame as though running toward
the loss we call the future and blood
sprouted like the little roses on her dress. All she wanted

was her grandmother's arms around her.
It's years later, of course, and that child
is a woman now, a woman who seems,
miraculously, to love me and is my friend, but still
when she's not looking, I watch her for signs

of despair, for the dark smudge of it
on her forehead where the scar from that first hurt

is barely visible, watch to see if I was a good teacher too.
In the film, the first thing we hear is a child
screaming just like my child screamed that day,
and the last thing we see is Majka's face
pressed against the window of a train, a scorched field
of loneliness, watching her daughter
run into her mother's arms. In my dreams I can't

tell if that face is mine or my mother's the last time
I saw her, driving away three days before her death.
It was Christmas, but there was some reproach
between us that day, its crimson lips pressed tight.
The morning she died, I rose up from a deep sleep
and in the dark I could hear the telephone waiting to ring.
I knew she was gone. Isn't that what I'd wanted all along?

The Old Testament

■

1. Genesis

April. The lilies rearing
their forked heads and wet clouds,
those dumb sheep, crouched
above the horizon. Sunday
and the long hours after church congealed
on the plate like the habitual roast and gravy.
Nap. Drive to the comic book store.
Nancy and Sluggo, adults pretending to be
children, or Archie and Veronica, children
pretending to be adults. Such privileged
childhoods, yet my sister hid in my mother's belly
and vowed never to come out, not in this life,
while the day crept uphill like water in a world
without gravity. Who could blame her?
Later, the sirens, the call. My cousin and his friend
playing cavalry, the word they always said wrong,
said *calvary*. And the rifle that was never loaded
was loaded. It put his eye out, my grandmother said,
and for hours it was as though that blue eye sat
in the middle of the kitchen table, atomic
and fierce, staring up at me. Could it have been
weeping? This was the boy who teased
till it bled, the family favorite, beautiful blue-eyed
boy who would be beautiful no longer.
The sun hissed and slithered away in the grass.
At the corner store, I asked for candy and told
what I knew, happy to be the bearer of bad news.

I was proud of it. This was the beginning.
And this is what knowledge brought me: sometimes
I still feel the snake curled deep inside me, squeezing

2. Exodus

"Bite her back!" my mother said. She held the neighbor
girl by the arms, and the girl cried and struggled
to get away. On my arm a tattoo of teeth
marks filling with blood. She'd tugged at it,
Amosandra, the "colored" baby doll, but I wouldn't
let go. Even when she bit me, I wouldn't
let go. And my mother, the same mother who always
told me never to hurt anyone, my mother
commanded me like God commanding Moses,
Nor must you show pity:
life for life, eye for eye,
tooth for tooth, hand for hand, foot for foot.
Elbow for elbow, she said. I feared
using my terrible powers, but what could I do?
The Law had spoken and I had to obey.
I bit her back then, same place, just below
the left elbow, doing the work the Lord ordained
and my mother—what did she do?—
my mother smiled and let her go.

Decalogue: Mothers and Sons

■

August, heat like a shroud
over the city, the ring
of ozone like a noose. Nothing
to do but stay inside.
The air conditioner squeals
like small animals trapped

in the walls. Nothing
to do but watch this movie,
this movie where the boy,
Tomek, a postal clerk, is obsessed
with an older woman and steals
a telescope to spy on her

across the courtyard, and she
lets him, makes sure
he sees her with her lovers.
Later, she'll take him home, she'll
humiliate him, he'll try to die
but will be saved by his landlady.

Oh, I can hardly watch,
there's such a whiff
of the Oedipal about it, odor
of cruelty and innocence at once.
It's not the same, of course,
but I have a son, a boy

who has three mothers: the girl
who gave birth to him, the stepmother,

and me, all of us leaving
barely a smudge
on the mirror, a soft
depression in his flesh.

Is this sentimental? That
I think every day of the day
I first saw him, sitting,
godlike, in a shaft of light and he
held up his arms to me? Every day
I think of the day he found me

gone, only empty hangers
in the closet and a single moth,
with her bright eyes, who wouldn't tell him
where I'd gone. Or why. What good
does it do him, my regret, regret
like a scar that never changes, never fades?

Once, passing a neighbor girl
he loved, he took my hand
and looked into my eyes and said,
"Mom, girls are really something."
I thought that was meant, at least
a little bit, for me.

He was afraid of bridges, my son.
Once, a little silver car
balanced atop a silver bridge,
while down below in the Chesapeake,
silver fish glinted like teeth. He hid his face
and wouldn't look until we'd crossed.

Once, I dreamed we drove
into a black cloud and stillness
and I put him in a ditch and covered
his small body with my own
until the tornado roared right over us.
For years I thought it really happened.

Once, on a city street, a cop
stopped me for jaywalking and I burst
into tears. I knew what I'd done
and I was inconsolable. He had
white-gloved hands like a mime.
"Never mind, lady," he said.

Oh, God, if you're out there,
what Commandments did I break?
I know I broke many. All.
Especially the unwritten one,
the one that should have read,
Honor thy children.

Tomek got his revenge.
It must have been sweet when Magda
came to him in the end and he told her
he no longer thought of her, sweet
the camera closing in on her, that final
zero of anguish on her face.

And for years my son wouldn't speak
to me. Who could blame him?
Once, on a day as hot as this one I stood
outside his door and pressed
the buzzer again and again and begged him
to let me in. He wouldn't answer.

And now? Now, years have passed.
Now we leave messages
on each other's answering machines,
tinny syllables cast out
into the air, cast out
into the future, into the past.

The Magic Hour

∎

In cinematography it's called *the magic hour,*
last full hour of the day, hour before night
swallows everything in its ravenous mouth,
hour when the light is warm, golden,
like bells pealing from St. Paul's, and the director
has maybe twenty minutes to send cameramen
and grips scurrying to set up the shot, to call
the beautiful actors from their trailers,
where maybe they are watching soaps or napping
or maybe making love, having fallen
into their roles, so he can shoot the scene
where the former lovers meet by chance
in the little park along the Thames,
he, walking his dog, she, hurrying head down
from an exhibition at the Tate, and when
they see each other after all these years,
their fate is irrevocable. Do you think
there was only one magic hour like that
in your life, one time you could have chosen
happiness and failed? Don't kid yourself.
There were many, the way if the scene's not right
this time, the director knows there will surely be
other days, other magic hours when the light lets down
its curtain of gauze over the stones, pink-streaked, blue.
But you, you seemed to miss them all.
Think of the thousands, no, millions of choices
in your life, all your sins of omission
and commission, the way you hoarded pieces
of yourself, little silver trinkets, as though they were
irreplaceable gold coins. Think of the Japanese man

you first saw at just such an hour
sitting on the mansion's terrace and the light
spread its wings and both of you
were lifted up, a man who loved you
so devotedly his devotion came to seem too much
and not enough, so that you sent him away forever.
Think of the husband you betrayed, the children,
the forgiveness you neither sought nor gave,
the regret that follows you, relentlessly, to your grave.

Decalogue: Ethics

■

Today is Yom Kippur and because there is no special day
of atonement for the skeptical and confused
I am at home alone watching this movie
and thinking, nevertheless, of the transgressions from *A* to *Z*:
we abuse, we betray, we are cruel, we destroy,
we embitter, we falsify . . . and of this
the Eighth Commandment: *Thou shalt not*
bear false witness against thy neighbor.

It's the child's face that haunts me, always
the child: eyes like muddy water after rain,
deep as a ditch with no bottom, ditch with hundreds
of bodies shoveled in, covered with cold rain.
Those eyes as she looks back at the woman
in the doorway and says, as though she knows a secret,
"Curfew time." But the woman just stands there. Forty years
she stands there and the child will remember everything.

They sat at the table and each china cup
had a different flower painted on it—rose, peony,
lily. The one she held, the lily, was chipped.
She was five, Warsaw, February 1943. In the ghetto
her father had long ago burned the dining room table.
Outside afternoon dimmed at the smoky windows,
the green oil lamp unlit. A young man, gray-faced, paced
up and down the small flat while the woman served tea

and an old man in a wheelchair kept his back to them,
picked at the blanket in his lap the way the dying do.
The child wanted more tea, but it was time to go.

"Curfew time," she said. They'd come
for the baptismal certificate—whatever that was,
something the goyim had—but the woman
wouldn't give it, had decided she couldn't lie,
couldn't bear false witness to Him in whom she believed,

she said. (Though, as someone would point out later,
any good Catholic would know saving a life
comes first—God would forgive that falsehood.)
At the gate the child looked back and swore
she'd never be afraid again. But now, forty years later,
she is, Elisabeth, an American now, sitting in the classroom
of the one who refused to help her, telling her story
as though it happened to someone else, offering it

as a problem for this ethics class—the subject
for the day is "ethical hell." She's come all this way
to see the professor's face. And the professor?
A cloud passes across that face, like a shadow
passing over a doorway. "Nothing is more important
than the life of a child," she says. We've seen her goodness
all along, the director makes it clear in the movie's
first frames, how kind her face, how wise,

when she's talking to her neighbor, buying flowers,
tidying her apartment. But how is one
to reconcile that goodness with the woman who turned
the child away? The explanation, after all, is almost
mundane, an ordinary, terrible wartime story: a rumor—
false, it turned out—that the Resistance was about to be
betrayed by Nazi sympathizers kept her from risking
the child's rescue. And she, of course, has long

believed she sent the child to certain death, has spent
a lifetime trying to atone for that moment in the doorway,
just as Elisabeth has spent one trying to understand it.
It's moving to see them there, these two,
in the lamplight of this simple Warsaw apartment,
late Soviet Warsaw, sharing their moment of reconciliation,
what Buber would call the *I-Thou*, the presence
of God. Some things remain mysterious.

The tailor, for instance, the one Zofia falsely believed a traitor,
simply stares and stays silent when she goes to his shop
forty years later. What are we to make of that?
The cold eye of justice? But that's not what pulls me back
to the film three times in one week. The professor has a son—
it's his old room in which she places flowers—lilies—every day.
They're estranged, we don't know why,
but when Elisabeth asks her where her son went,

she says, "Quite simply, far away from me."
And perhaps that's some kind of retribution
for turning away a child in the five o'clock dark
of Noakowski Street, in February 1943. Perhaps
she turned her heart away from her own child
out of guilt, or self-loathing, maybe, couldn't give him
what she thought she had denied another. I'll never know.
I have a son whom I betrayed, who now seems lost

to me. It was winter and dark. I turned away
and left him standing in an empty house, and now
he is showing me how it feels to be left like that.
In the movie inside me, the one I rewind again and again,
he runs into the house, five years old, his eyes
black and muddy, he's looking for me everywhere,

wants to tell me about the battlefield, Gettysburg,
he's seen that day. He waves his toy rifle in the air.

But I'm not there. I will never be there again.
Nothing is more important than the life of a child.
Near the end of the film, Zofia, the professor,
says she doesn't try to teach her students
how to live, but how to discover it for themselves.
Why? Elizabeth asks. *Because goodness exists*
in all of us, that is what God is, Zofia says,
but people are free to choose, to leave God behind.

And instead of Him? *Loneliness,*
here and there. Try to think it out to the end.
If there is nothing but emptiness, if it is
emptiness indeed, then. . . .
And if to save one life is to save the world, I think,
then is to lose one life to lose everything?
To forgive oneself is a work that never ends, every day
cutting lilies, putting them in a cheap crockery jar.

Horoscope

■

It's almost my birthday, but not quite, thank God, because
who'd want a horoscope like this on her birthday?

Take precautions today. Evil may come your way.
Because evil is such an over-the-top word, such

a nightmare-on-elm-street word. I mean, it could've said,
"Trouble may come your way," but evil? Not that

I don't believe in it, of course. Who wouldn't these days?
Decades of it, centuries. Hitler, Pol Pot, Saddam,

the usual suspects, not to mention countless other lackeys
and minor functionaries, the father who scalded the baby,

put out his cigarettes on her tender backside, the loser boyfriend
who shot the aspiring actress right in front of her mother

on a sidewalk in Chinatown. Or the serial killer everyone describes
as "polite" and "charming," whose face is all over the TV today,

the one who haunted south Louisiana through which I have so often
traveled alone, driving over the spooky swamp between Lafayette

and Baton Rouge, where there is no way off the interstate for miles
except the exit at Whiskey Bay, where one of the bodies

was found, haunted even Breaux Bridge, where the Sunday
after Christmas I ate crawfish etoufée at Mulate's Original Cajun Restaurant,

the band playing at one o'clock in the afternoon and couples
in matching outfits dancing the day away. Oh, I could go on

and on. Some days the grease of grief covers everything,
a thin film like the one that covers the body in the river. Yesterday

my friend, the most beautiful woman I know, was speaking
of sadness, and just for a moment I thought if I were

that beautiful I'd never be sad about anything, but then
I felt ashamed because I know sadness

is an equal-opportunity emotion and despair
can lead you around by the nose no matter who you are.

Remember when we were so avid for life we beat like little moths
around the days as though they were shining lamps?

Now, some days, I think merely to get up,
to make coffee and take the dog out into the May morning, to put

your face up close to the pink face of the odorless, frustrating
hibiscus is an act of endless courage. But last night

at a party I held a baby for an hour and he curled into me
like a new leaf, and today there is a family of cardinals

in the Japanese maple and nearby a mockingbird barking and cackling
and dive-bombing the gray cat, who would eat the baby birds if he could.

And he could. And still the mockingbird will go on singing
in the privet hedge the whole May night. I can think of that couple

at Mulate's, their white shirts embroidered all over with red poinsettias.
Imagine her bending over her needle night after night and the tender way

he puts his palm on her back when they dance. And I have the memory
of my handsome young man of a son striding toward me

across Union Station, Baltimore, and his face when he sees me
and sweeps me up, apparently having forgotten all the reasons he had not to

speak to me last year. Nearby a covey of teenage girls keeps looking
his way, a little like newly hatched birds themselves, all legs and eyes,

despite their bare midriffs and lowrider cutoffs. Caleb just laughs.
"When I have daughters," he says, taking my arm, "they'll wear

baggy jeans and big T-shirts that say *I love my daddy*, and they'll always
love me best." They won't, of course, but for now

I can dream these girls are his girls and have come with him
to the train station to meet me, the one who has traveled far into the future

just to see them, these girls who beat around us
like those moths around lamps, their wings little sparks of flame.

Without Number

■

Today at the stop sign by the cemetery I counted
twenty cars in the two minutes or so I waited,
some with more than one person inside,
at the bookstore maybe five or six people,
at the coffee shop seven, at the grocery store
maybe twelve, not to mention the people I passed
on the sidewalk, the ones in other cars I didn't count, and this
in the space of an hour. I wondered how many more
living souls I'd cross paths with in my life, a number
too vast to imagine. If I laid each body head to foot,
how far would they stretch? Across the country?
Around the globe? So many lives, each with longing
deep inside like a held breath. Whole armies of the jilted,
the brokenhearted, bearing their hearts in front of them
like shields or questions: *Can you see me? Can you see me?*
So many sick, so many dying, the grieving
without number, the poor without number, the hungry, the abused.
But so much happiness, too, surely, even joy, and right now
I want to talk about that, to keep the world's sorrows
at bay, if only for a while. The happiness, for instance,
of the tourist couple with their ice-cream cones,
and when she finishes hers, he buys her another
because she can't make up her mind which flavor
she likes best, and the ocean spreads its blue light
over everything. Or the boy in the Red Sox cap
outside the bakery, Friday afternoon and a long holiday
weekend ahead, baseball playoffs on TV.
And me at lunch with my friend the chaplain, his sweet face
lit up across the table, not caring whether or not
I'm a believer, and the good talk we talk so that sometimes
I imagine I can see his heart glowing beneath his suit,

the suit he says makes him look like an FBI agent.
So much happiness, lovers without number, music,
children among flowers in a painting by Sargent at the Tate,
blue sole on a blue plate and the bottle of wine you splurged on
just to celebrate living. The friend who, when you're sad,
knows how you feel, and why. Or that hot August night
in Cortona, the hottest summer in history
the Italians said, so many bodies pressed into the small square
it was like hundreds of bodies stacked in one coffin, Nigerian boys
hawking fake Fendi bags at the edge of the crowd, and then
the gospel singers began to sing, their large, American voices
bouncing off the medieval buildings, their black faces
blue in the klieg lights, their red dresses flashing
heat lightning across the stage, and everyone,
even the ones who didn't know the language, who didn't know
the music, its shouts and moans, its Hallelujahs and Amens,
everyone began to dance in her own inch of space, everyone
began to sing, to shout, touching elbows
with those beside them, and the sweaty moon went on shining
in the sweaty night, shining over the Piazza Republica,
over the hundreds of bodies, a thousand maybe, bodies
that seemed to move as one body, and everyone of us,
believers, nonbelievers, everyone seemed blessed.
And today, too, when I turned for home down Buttonwood Road
and a doe and her fawn floated out of the pines and she leapt
in front of my car as if to force me to stop till the fawn
disappeared out of sight, and I stopped.
She was so lovely, so perfect in her *doeness*, that I held my breath
for a moment while we looked straight into each other's eyes,
both of us, I think, a little afraid.
It seemed like minutes passed, though it was probably seconds.
I wanted so much to reach right through the windshield,
to take her in my arms and hold her close, wanted
to whisper that I meant her no harm. And then she was gone.

Decalogue: Chance

∎

It's May, birthday month, daylily month, and here's one
called "Artist at Work"—pale yellow segments
with a dark red throat. *Hemerocallis,* "beauty for a day."
Too easy to say our lives are like that, blooming once, flaring up,
going out, like candles on a cake, the chocolate one

my mother baked each birthday. Lately they seem
more like children, some bratty Dick and Jane sticking their tongues out,
waving to us from the back window of a long, black car—Goodbye!
Goodbye!—while we wipe away the tears.
How random the world has seemed, despite the daylily's scarlet throat,

its 52,000 varieties. The news like fat hands around a slender neck—
a shooting at a school, tornadoes in Oklahoma scattering houses like so many
leaves, while passengers fell from a plane over the Congo, not to mention
war in Afghanistan. And the film I watched last night
was hardly a comfort, full of violence and despair. I saw then how

anyone could be the cabdriver who picks up the murderer
or the one who drives on by, you could be the murderer's
little sister run over by a drunken tractor or the girls
who smile in the pictures he sees in the photo shop.
That's the director's point, I guess. Sure, we've all had

close calls—not just the public ones, the Cuban
Missile Crisis, but pneumonia that tried to smother me
throughout my childhood, turn my lungs to paper. The stranger
who followed me twenty miles home and drove off
when he saw I was eight months pregnant. Even late last night

when I smelled smoke and found the lampshade by my bed
about to burst into flame. Think of all the times the truck
swerved just in time, the car ran the red light just after I passed.
And there are moments so ablaze with grace they shine in the dark
like a whole garden of daylilies, like the story a friend told once,

a group of us sitting on the porch in the ample lap of July
talking about our childhoods, the ones we survived and those
we didn't. My friend said at twelve he came home early from school
and found his mother in the basement weeping and never knew why.
Years later she told him she'd been about to kill herself

when he walked in and then she didn't. Some say God's grace,
not chance. Does it matter? All I know is that there are little moments, too,
when things seem to go your way. Today for instance, Graduation Day
at the college where I teach, but when I went to pick up my cap and gown,
there wasn't anything with my name on it and so I was excused

from going, this bright May day, when it was 82 degrees
and 80 percent humidity at 8 a.m.—did I mention that graduation
is always held outdoors? And that's how I came to be sitting
here this morning, ogling the daylilies, their red lips,
their pink tongues, happy, for once, to have the chance.

My Mother Comes Back to Me

■

That's where it all began, the minute
the theater lights went down and the screen
lit up, the child's eyes shimmering with tears,
single-minded as grief this task of trying
to suck her thumb, arm and hand
encased in plaster, and her father saying, *Mommy*
was broken, they might not be able to
fix her, so we know she's already dead
when he draws a dog on the child's cast.
That's when my tears began, sometimes
leaking from behind my eyelids, etching
their tracks down my cheeks like scratches
from brambles, rainwater cupping
into my hands, and sometimes they came
in gulps, in sobs, in gullies, the way Ponette waits
so stubbornly for her mother to return and blames
herself until she wants to die, flinging herself
face down in the dirt dug from her mother's grave,
as though if she could just see inside it
she could meet her mother coming
or going and disappear forever
to where her mother disappeared. She thinks
God must be angry, her mother must be angry.
The children in the schoolyard are just like us, so full
of certainty, of misinformation, about the dead,
about God, that Ponette must prove her bravery
again and again—tests of the playground,
dark of the dumpster, the vigil at her mother's grave—

before she's offered at last a vision of happiness.
My mother dead for thirteen years, I cried
straight through to the movie's last astonishing moment,
so that when the mother—ghost or wish?—comes back
to ask Ponette to promise she'll taste every single thing
and only die alive and shows her how to pluck memories
from the air at will, I was still afraid, somehow,
to lose my sadness. Later, though, sitting outside
under an August sky the color of blue hydrangeas,
a few white clouds beating their wings above me,
I watched my friend cut open a watermelon, its pink flesh,
its bright red heart salty and sweet at once, and then
out of the bright air my mother came back to me:
The cricket-filled dusk of a summer night and my mother
and her sister are trying to carry a watermelon
from a neighbor's house to ours. I don't know why,
where the men are, but my cousins and I dance
around them like fireflies, our bodies sticky
with heat, and I remember my mother's dress,
its sprigs of roses, damp scent of Chanel No. 5.
She's not yet forty, lovely still, though she doesn't believe it,
brushing her bangs from her eyes, and the women
are laughing, laughing because the melon is so heavy
they can take only a few steps without stopping to rest.
At this rate, my mother says, it's going to be rotten
before we get it across the street, and for some reason
this seems so funny to them that my aunt tells my mother
to stop, she's going to pee her pants, she swears to goodness—
she'd never say God—and they laugh even more, so much
that my aunt drops her end of the melon and my mother
does too, drops her end, so there's a kind of thud
when the melon hits the pavement, my mother sitting down

now on top of it right there in the middle of the street,
laughing so hard she's crying, her body
convulsed with laughter, until at last I see her face
shining up at me through the pure joy of tears.

Decalogue: Siblings

■

The dour director has saved the comic
for last, a kind of sorbet to cleanse the palate
after a heavy meal, perhaps, or a show of bravery
against all the evidence, the way my little pug
scratches the ground like a bull and barks
at the last of the black-eyed Susans tossing
their pretty heads in the wind. Maybe he means to say
that although we alone of all the animals are doomed
to know our fate, there's humor here, and love.
It's a kind of fairy tale, really, a kind of zany

riff on the Brothers Grimm, this story
of two hapless brothers who inherit their father's
valuable stamp collection, while in the background
the members of one brother's rock band screech
out a song that begins, "Kill, kill, kill!"
When they try to sell the stamps, of course
complications ensue. One of them, Artur, takes
the most valuable stamps, the "Zeppelins," ignorant
of their worth, to give to Jerzy's son, who likes airplanes.
When they find a rare stamp their father coveted, a stamp

which will make the collection even more valuable,
the only way the stamp merchant will sell it
is if Jerzy donates a kidney to save his dying daughter,
like some medieval test the prince must pass to win the princess,
and while he's in the hospital, the stamps are stolen, and what's more,
the big black dog the brothers bought to guard the collection

just sits there quietly and lets the robbers take everything!
You get the picture. In the end, each of the brothers
goes off to buy new stamps and returns home
to find they've bought exactly the same ones.

All they're left with is a newfound love
of stamp collecting. And each other, of course.
I envied them that. While the final credits rolled,
the bad rock song came back with its lyrics
of "Kill, kill, kill, screw who you will, lust and crave,
pervert and deprave every day of the week . . . "
as if in some kind of ironic commentary
on the director's gloomy oeuvre. I had to laugh
at that, of course, but it was bittersweet.
By the time I had turned off the movie, it had begun

to rain, last of a hurricane with an old-fashioned name,
Jeanne, opening her mouth and spewing her anger all over
the island, her fists beating the black-eyed Susans,
pummeling the hydrangeas—so unladylike,
our mother would've said. Then you, little sister,
who never had a name, came to visit me
in my solitary house. You were angry too, angry
because I'd had a life and you hadn't, the way
I've been angry at you for dying and leaving me alone
with them all those years. Sure, I was jealous,

but I would have gotten over it. If you'd been there,
I could have tied your sash and braided your hair, shooed
the spider off your pillow and taken your hand and run
when the man in the pickup asked you to help
find his dog. I could have shown you how to play canasta
with Granny, the hiding place under the honeysuckle,

the mimosa where I had an epiphanic experience
(though I don't know if that's even a word, *epiphanic*).
And later I could have told you all I knew
about boys, which wasn't much, and dances

at the Hut on Saturday nights, and how
it was okay if no one asked you to dance.
But they would. Later we could have had
marriages together, babies together, maybe
even divorces. We could have chucked it all
and flown off to Italy to sit at that little café
by the park in Cortona and drink cheap Chianti
and watch the endless passeggiata of beautiful boys
and girls, girls balancing on the highest heels
we'd ever seen. We could have taken the train to Rome

and a small apartment above Il Sogno, the toy store,
where we could hear the expensive dolls
talking to each other all night, and if we couldn't sleep,
we'd go down to the Piazza Navona, where
the same fortuneteller has sat at the same table
for thirty-seven years, and every night she'd tell us
the same fortune—love and money—and we'd act
surprised. We could have traded lovers then
or spurned men altogether, who knows?
I've missed you. Have you missed me?

Gratification

∎

You're walking through the woods toward Sepiessa Point,
you and the dog, late September, late afternoon, late light
leafing through its book of trees—pitch pine and beetlebung,
scrub oak, the understory all huckleberry like a good plot,
tangled, dark, and bittersweet. You're happy enough,
biding your time. Over there, by Tiah's Cove,
some farmer staked his happiness. See,
even his fence extends a foot or two into the water
to keep his goats from drowning. From a high pole,
an osprey jumps feet first into the cove like a kid
jumping off the high board for the first time. And suddenly,
the trees fall off, the sand plain opens up and there it is,
Tisbury Great Pond, and beyond it the Atlantic,
going who knows where, and the water
is an improbable blue, like the blue in the windows
at Chartres, a blue no one has ever been able
to reproduce, but here it is. You can barely see
what keeps them apart, the pond and the ocean,
but in the distance is a little strip of beach. And sometimes
it wears away, or someone digs it out, and the ocean
enters the pond at last. In the deep sand
Cosmo the pug staggers like a happy drunk, charges
the water, eyes the merganser rasping
his old smoker's croak. Every time, arriving here
is a surprise, like getting what you've always wanted
but never thought you'd have—the last piece
of peach pie, all the first editions of your favorite writer—
not to sell, just to keep—that longed-for kiss, someone

knowing, *really knowing*, just how you feel. Now
the sun is going down in flames like a ship
on fire, but slowly, listing a little to the left.
Don't worry, everyone on board gets off.
That's the best part. Everyone is saved.

Elegy for My Pug Cosmo

I wanted an abacus to count my failures, though maybe they were too many to
    count,
like marbles in a glass jar—guess the number and win a prize, No Regrets or
    Eternal Life,
take your pick. One with your name on it, your ugly, beautiful pug face on it,

a face about which a child once asked, "Why does Cosmo always look like he's mad?"
But you were hardly ever mad, just sad, sometimes, when I wasn't there, maybe,
or when the bully cat Lily stared you off a pillow. And so I keep on telling myself

there was no way off the freeway and us marooned in our oven-baked car
running from Hurricane Rita—though no one was going anywhere,
eight hours to go eight miles—Rita, with her sexy, tropical name, a name as dated

as red-haired Rita Hayworth in *Miss Sadie Thompson* (Columbia, 1953),
that sultry voice saying, "Look at that sky, as if not a thing was going on under it,"
and the sky looked like that, blue, almost cloudless, though the radio said the
    storm

was coming, thousands of us going nowhere, beat-up pickups, Benzes, my
    practical Civic,
all locked nose to tail like a herd of dumb cattle, another failure of imagination—
Brownie, you're doin' a heckuva job—though not as costly as Katrina, not as deadly,

only—only!—a few elderly heat-felled, plus twenty-three more from a nursing
    home
burned up in a bus crash, several pets. Forgive me, but this seems to be a metaphor,
all of us fleeing our fears, fears which might not even be real, until we get stuck

in those fears and can't move and even worse things happen. What is it that keeps us
from going another way, from finding that one exit ramp and getting off
the hopeless road when we have a chance? I wish I knew. I wish I knew why I
   couldn't

see how futile this was, that the lanes were never going to open up and give us
the perfect escape route we wanted, long before you began to pant and gasp and
   pace
the backseat, long before your steadfast heart gave out. I couldn't save you then.

I tell myself that's what I was trying to do, but, really, your death seemed another
   failure
in my long list of failures, another small being I couldn't protect or save.
Now your ashes in a red velvet box on my bookshelf. Next summer I'll scatter them

on the Vineyard at the places you loved best, Sepiessa Point and the beach
at Lambert's Cove, where you and your dachshund friend Lucky—dead now, too—
never tired of barking at waves. And maybe I've carried my failures around too long,

carried them around like marbles in a glass jar, trying to count them, to go over
and over them, as if that would tell me anything I didn't know, carried them around
like a little box of ashes I could cradle in my arms and sing to in the night,

as if that would comfort me. I don't think I want to carry them anymore.
I think I'd like to let them go now, just float away, scattered like ashes, ashes
slowly sifting through my fingers onto the blue, translucent surface of the water.

Acknowledgments

Thanks to the editors of the following publications in which these poems appeared, sometimes in slightly different form:

American Poetry Review: "*Decalogue:* Mothers and Sons" and "*Decalogue:* Mothers and Daughters"

Five Points: "Gratification," "The Soul Bone," "A Short History of Women in the Nineteenth Century," and "The Old Testament"

Georgia Review: "My Mother Comes Back to Me," "*Decalogue:* Thin Ice," "*Decalogue:* What If," and "*Decalogue:* Ethics"

Greensboro Review: "If Grief Were a Bird"

Gulf Coast: "*Decalogue:* Chance" and "*Decalogue:* Fathers and Daughters"

Kenyon Review: "*Decalogue:* Husbands and Wives" and "Soledad" (as part of a longer poem, "Leafing")

Meridian: "*Decalogue:* Rooms"

New England Review: "The Lord God Returns"

Northwest Review: "My Father Looks Down on Me," "The Magic Hour," "Palace Theater," and "Dotage"

Smartish Pace: "Custody," "Without Number," "*Decalogue:* Siblings," "Elegy for My Pug Cosmo"

TriQuarterly: "Horoscope" and "I Got a Mind to Ramble"

Virginia Quarterly Review: "In America"

"After His Retirement, LBJ Visits Greenville" and "The Strange Case of the Virgin Lidwina," first appeared in *Callaloo* 32:1 (Winter 2009): 138–41. Copyright 2009, Charles H. Rowell. Reprinted with permission by The Johns Hopkins University Press.

"Gratification" was reprinted in *Best American Poetry 2006*—thanks to Billy Collins.

"The Lord God Returns" also appeared on *Poetry Daily* and was nominated by the *New England Review* for a Pushcart Prize, receiving an honorable mention. Thanks to C. Dale Young.

"Horoscope" was reprinted in *Seriously Funny,* edited by Barbara Hamby and David Kirby (University of Georgia Press, 2010). Thanks to Barbara and David.

"A Short History of Women in the Nineteenth Century" and "The Old Testament" received the 2009 James Dickey Prize in Poetry from *Five Points: A Journal of Literature and the Arts.* Thanks to Megan Sexton and David Bottoms.

My gratitude to the friends who read some of these poems in manuscript form and offered sage advice: Jericho Brown, Steve Gehrke, Tony Hoagland, Steve Orlen, Stanley Plumley, Marsha Recknagel, Suzanne Rindell, Sasha West, and, especially, Barbara Hamby. Thanks again to Letha Cole for her tough-minded encouragement and wisdom over many years. Thanks to Susan Shreve and Timothy Seldes for their long friendship and for loaning me their house on Martha's Vineyard, and thanks to Rice University and former dean of Humanities Gary Wihl for allowing me generous leave to work on this book. And thanks to Caleb, Caitlin, Martha and Orly, who mean everything to me.

I'd like to express my thanks to my editor at the University of Pittsburgh Press, Ed Ochester, and to others there who made this book better than it would have been without them, particularly Kelley Hope Johovic, Maria Sticco, Ann Walston, Alex Wolfe, and Chiquita Babb.

Notes

The epigraph is from the Polish film director Krzysztof Kieslowski, first quoted in *Kieslowski on Kieslowski,* edited by Danusia Stok (Faber and Faber, 1993).

The *"Decalogue"* poems had their genesis in Kieslowski's *Dekalog*, ten short films originally made for Polish television in 1988. The films are, in one sense, Kieslowski's meditation on the Ten Commandments, though they do not follow a strict order, nor is any one film necessarily limited to reflecting only one Commandment. As Kieslowski noted, his films are as much concerned with sins against oneself as they are sins against whatever we mean when we say "God." The speaker of these poems uses the films to address her own struggles to understand the nature of God, sin, and death.

"I Got a Mind to Ramble" is for Julia Markus. Alberta Hunter, the American blues singer and songwriter, born in 1895, achieved fame in the 1920s and 1930s and was best known for the songs "Downhearted Blues" and "My Man Is Such a Handy Man." In 1954 Hunter retired from show business, spending more than twenty years as a nurse in New York City, and her remarkable singing was largely forgotten. In 1978 Bernard Josephson persuaded her to sing at his Greenwich Village nightclub, The Cookery, where she immediately became a media sensation, was signed by Columbia Records, and continued to appear at The Cookery until just before her death in October 1984.

"The Strange Case of the Virgin Lidwina": The title is from a fifteenth-century document describing the illness of St. Lidwina, which is believed to be the earliest known recorded case of the illness we now call multiple sclerosis. This poem is for Marsha Recknagel.

"Horoscope" is for Barbara Hamby and David Kirby.

"Gratification" is for Orly.